Ulysses S. Grant
18th U.S. President

18

Written by **Joeming Dunn**   Illustrated by **Rod Espinosa**

magic
Wagon

visit us at www.abdopublishing.com

Published by Magic Wagon, a division of the ABDO Publishing Group, 8000 West 78th Street, Edina, Minnesota 55439. Copyright © 2012 by Abdo Consulting Group, Inc. International copyrights reserved in all countries. All rights reserved. No part of this book may be reproduced in any form without written permission from the publisher.

Graphic Planet™ is a trademark and logo of Magic Wagon.

Printed in the United States of America, North Mankato, Minnesota.
042011
092011
This title contains at least 10% recycled materials.

Written by Joeming Dunn
Illustrated and colored by Rod Espinosa
Lettered by Rod Espinosa
Edited by Stephanie Hedlund and Rochelle Baltzer
Interior layout and design by Antarctic Press
Cover art by Rod Espinosa
Cover design by Abbey Fitzgerald

Library of Congress Cataloging-in-Publication Data

Dunn, Joeming W.
  Ulysses S. Grant : 18th U.S. president / written by Joeming Dunn ; illustrated by Rod Espinosa.
    p. cm. -- (Presidents of the United States bio-graphics)
  ISBN 978-1-61641-646-1
  1. Grant, Ulysses S. (Ulysses Simpson), 1822-1885--Juvenile literature. 2. Presidents--United States--Biography--Juvenile literature. 3. Generals--United States--Biography--Juvenile literature. 4. United States. Army--Biography--Juvenile literature. 5. Grant, Ulysses S. (Ulysses Simpson), 1822-1885--Comic books, strips, etc. 6. Presidents--United States--Biography--Comic books, strips, etc. 7. Generals--United States--Biography--Comic books, strips, etc. 8. United States. Army--Biography--Comic books, strips, etc. 9. Graphic novels. I. Espinosa, Rod, ill. II. Title.
  E672.D86 2012
  973.8'2092--dc22
  [B]
                                        2011010676

Table of Contents

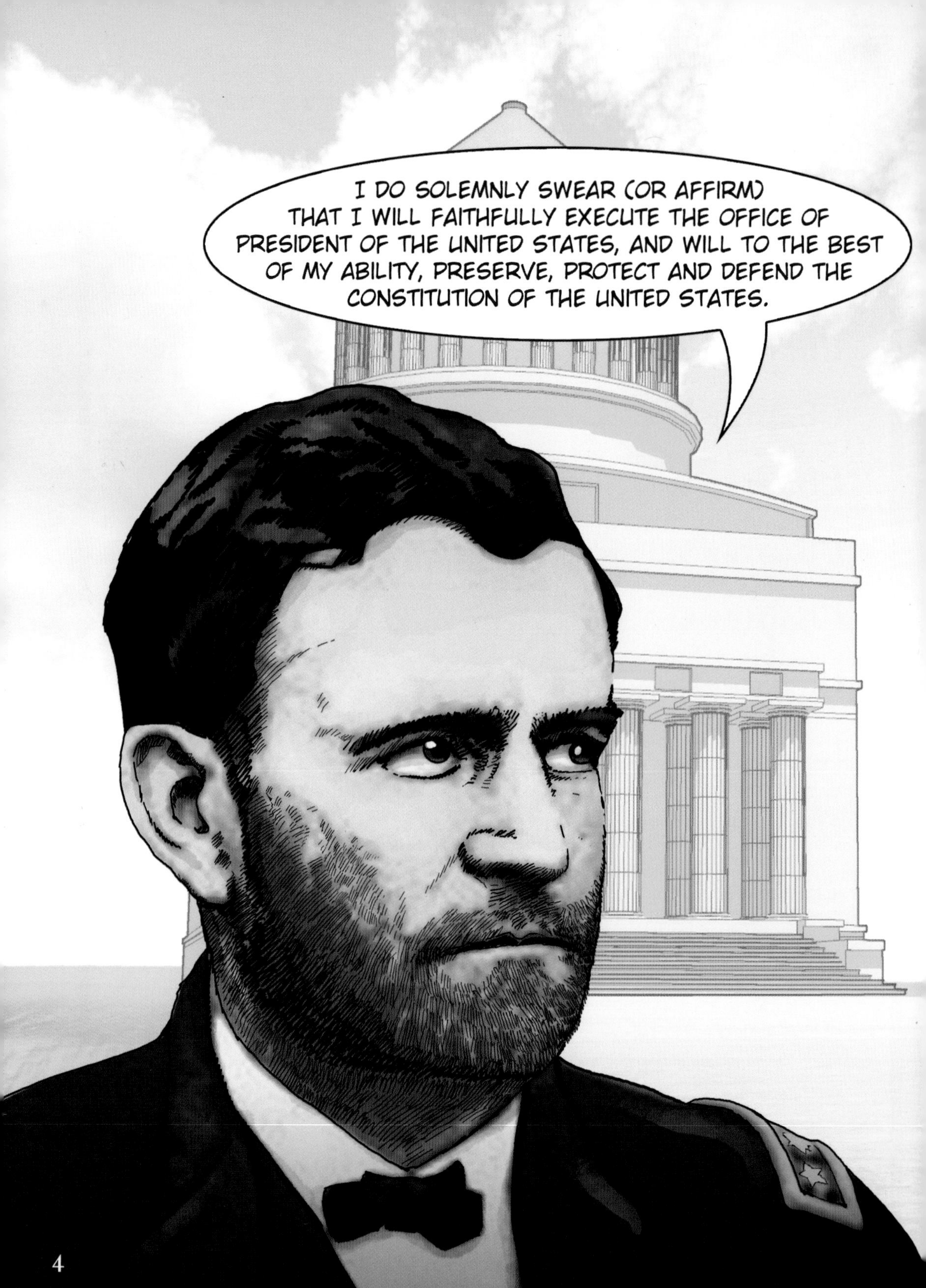
I DO SOLEMNLY SWEAR (OR AFFIRM) THAT I WILL FAITHFULLY EXECUTE THE OFFICE OF PRESIDENT OF THE UNITED STATES, AND WILL TO THE BEST OF MY ABILITY, PRESERVE, PROTECT AND DEFEND THE CONSTITUTION OF THE UNITED STATES.

Chapter 1:
Ulysses S. Grant

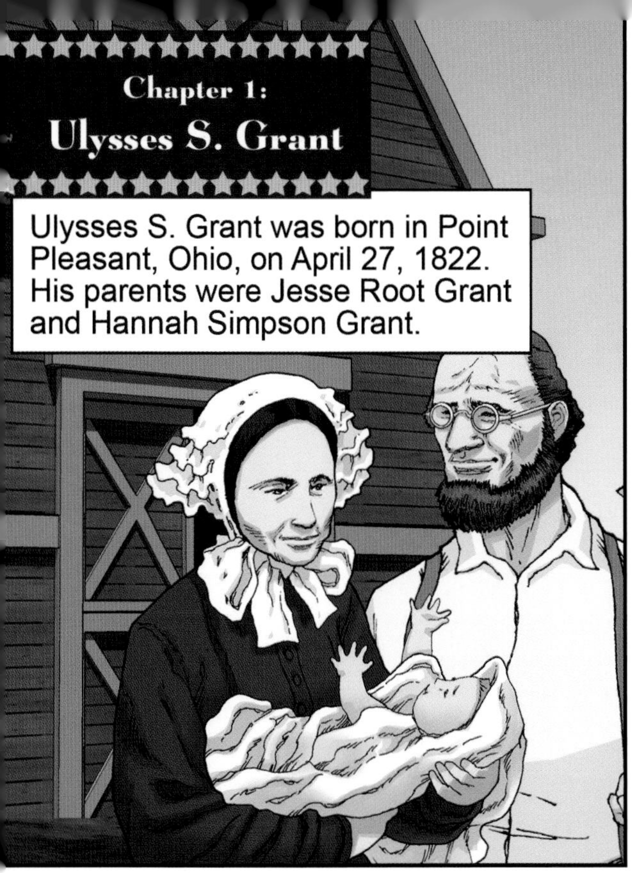
Ulysses S. Grant was born in Point Pleasant, Ohio, on April 27, 1822. His parents were Jesse Root Grant and Hannah Simpson Grant.

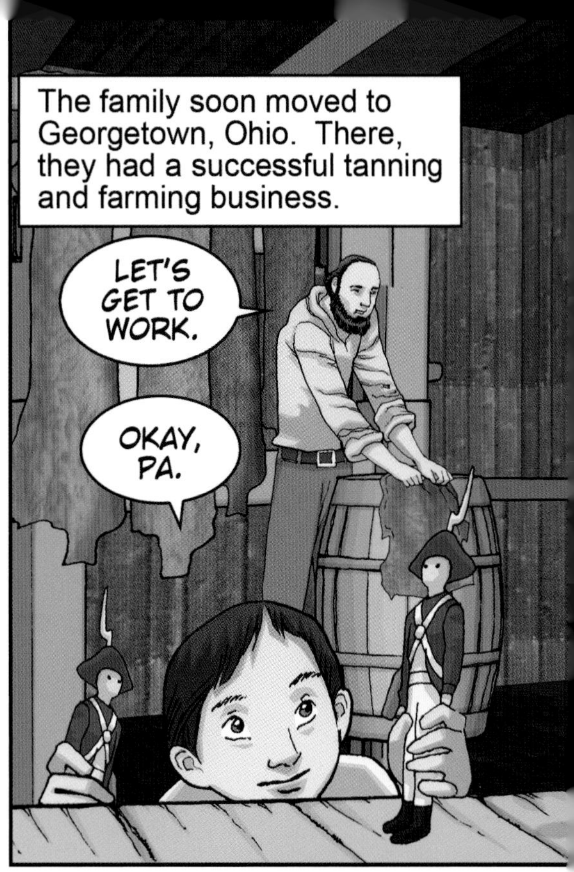
The family soon moved to Georgetown, Ohio. There, they had a successful tanning and farming business.
LET'S GET TO WORK.
OKAY, PA.

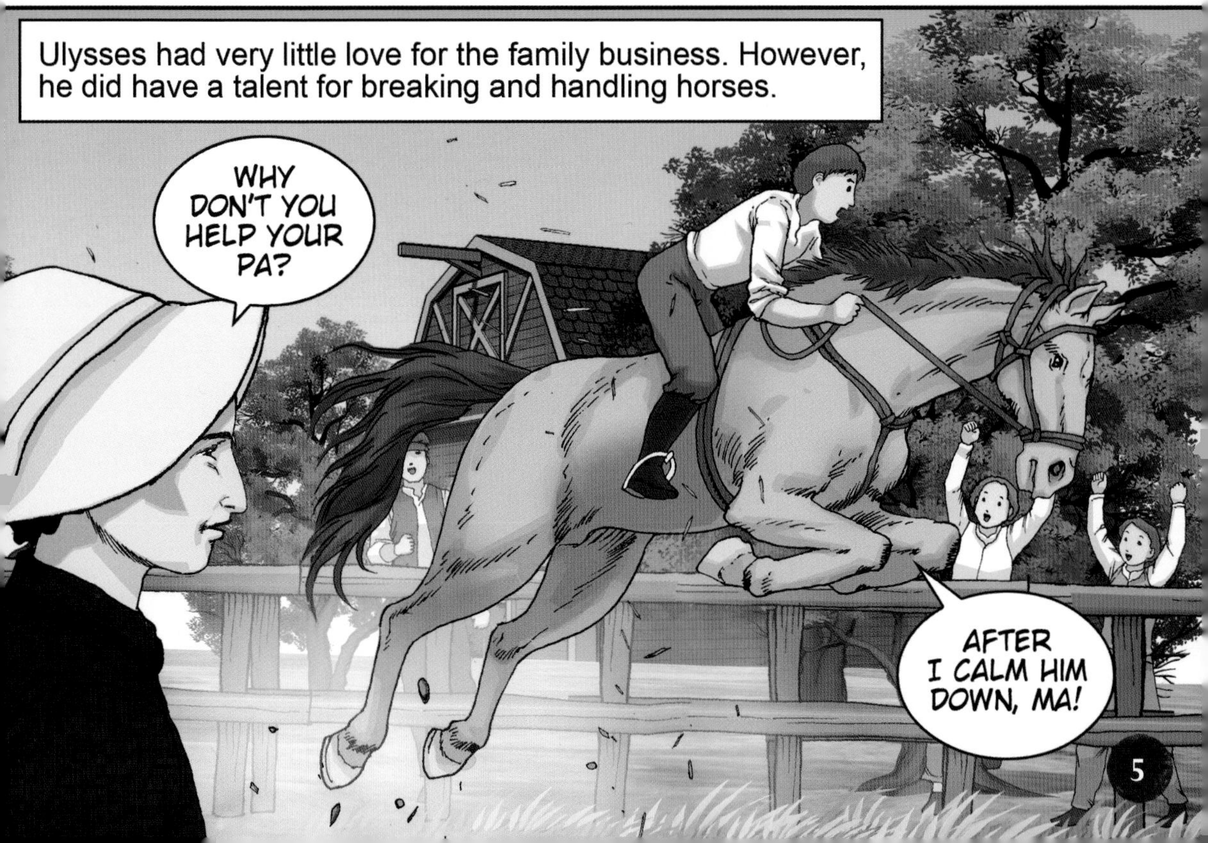
Ulysses had very little love for the family business. However, he did have a talent for breaking and handling horses.
WHY DON'T YOU HELP YOUR PA?
AFTER I CALM HIM DOWN, MA!

In 1839, Jesse helped Ulysses get into the United States Military Academy at West Point, New York.

Ulysses was not the best student. But, he did well in mathematics and horsemanship.

Originally, he had hoped to be a math teacher at West Point.

But upon graduation, he was assigned to the 4th U.S. Infantry near St. Louis, Missouri.

6

He served under the command of General Zachary Taylor.

From 1846 to 1848, they fought together during the Mexican War. Grant learned military strategy during this time.

Grant was then given a new position. He was in charge of all of the supplies for the troops of General Winfield Scott.

Grant proved himself in battle. He received two awards for bravery, but he was personally against war.

Over the next several years, Grant was given posts in New York, Michigan, and the Oregon Territory. He became captain in August 1853 and then was sent to Fort Humboldt in California.

In St. Louis, Grant met Julia Boggs Dent. They married in 1848.

Grant left the army on April 11, 1854. He returned to St. Louis. There, he took up farming land given to him and Julia by her parents.

Even with great effort, farming was too difficult. The farm soon failed.

Grant then got into the leather goods business owned by his father in Galena, Illinois.

In April 1861, the Confederate States of America attacked Fort Sumter. This started the Civil War.

President Abraham Lincoln called for volunteers to fight in the war.

Grant quit his job and put on his military uniform. He began organizing a company of volunteers from Galena.

Governor Richard Yates saw Grant's abilities. He put Grant to work in the office that organized, trained, and supplied the volunteers.

Soon, Grant became colonel and was given the 21st Illinois Volunteers to command. At the time, this was a very unruly regiment. Grant's job was to whip this regiment into shape.

He was very successful. President Lincoln heard of Grant's success.

On August 7, 1861, President Lincoln made him brigadier general of the volunteers at Cairo, Illinois.

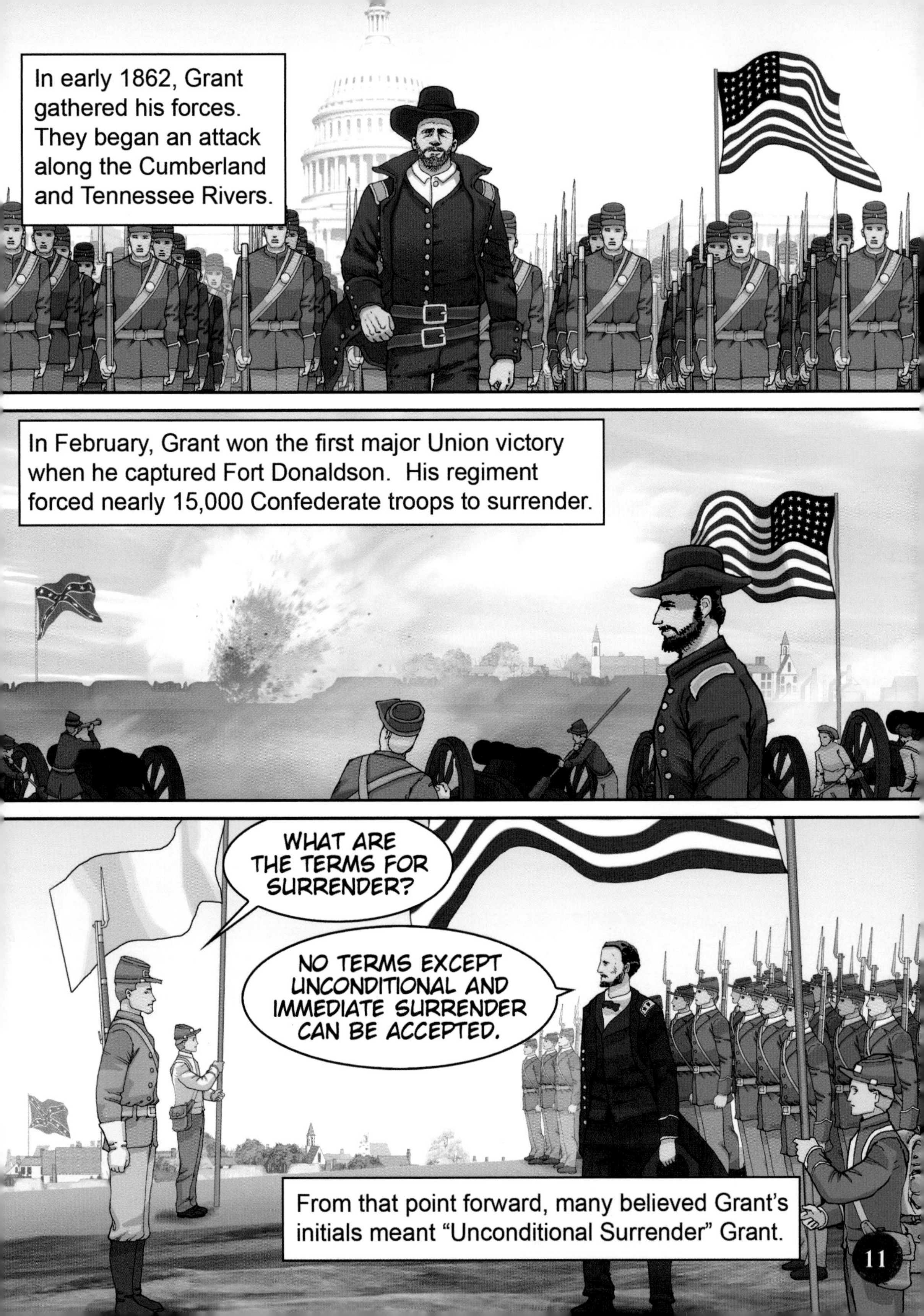
In early 1862, Grant gathered his forces. They began an attack along the Cumberland and Tennessee Rivers.
In February, Grant won the first major Union victory when he captured Fort Donaldson. His regiment forced nearly 15,000 Confederate troops to surrender.
WHAT ARE THE TERMS FOR SURRENDER?
NO TERMS EXCEPT UNCONDITIONAL AND IMMEDIATE SURRENDER CAN BE ACCEPTED.
From that point forward, many believed Grant's initials meant "Unconditional Surrender" Grant.

Grant was then named major general.

On April 6, 1862, the Confederates attacked Union lines. They were at the Shiloh Church in Pittsburg Landing, Tennessee.

There were many Union losses from the battle.

Due to the number of lives lost, some urged Lincoln to remove Grant from command. In the end, Grant kept his position.

I CAN'T SPARE THIS MAN--HE FIGHTS.

At the end of 1862, Grant continued his advance along the Mississippi River.

When his army was cut off from Union supplies and communication, Grant surrounded Vicksburg, Mississippi. This was a Confederate fort. The six-week siege eventually led to a Confederate surrender and the capture of 30,000 troops in July 1863.

Union troops continued marching down to Port Hudson, Louisiana. They captured the last Confederate post along the Mississippi River. This cut the Confederacy in half.

Grant became a hero throughout the North.

President Lincoln then named Grant commander of the Western armies. Later, he was made lieutenant general and supreme commander of all the Union forces.

Grant was able to win a major battle at Chattanooga, Tennessee. This opened the doors for an invasion of the South.

He sent General Philip Sheridan to destroy the supply and communication lines in Virginia.

Meanwhile, General William Sherman was sent to capture Savannah, Georgia. This campaign is also known as Sherman's March to the Sea.

General Robert E. Lee and his army were soon surrounded by Union troops at Petersburg, Virginia. They later surrendered to the Union at Appomattox Court House in Virginia.

Grant was again a hero. He was very popular.

He was given houses and money as gifts for his fine work.

In 1866, Grant was given the rank of full general of the army. At the time, he was only the second person to earn that rank, following George Washington.

On April 14, 1865, President Lincoln was assassinated by John Wilkes Booth.

After Lincoln's death, Andrew Johnson became the seventeenth president of the United States.

Together, Grant and Johnson oversaw the period of Reconstruction in the South.

Edwin M. Stanton was secretary of war under Abraham Lincoln. He remained in that position under Andrew Johnson. Johnson and Stanton disagreed on how to treat the South during Reconstruction, so Johnson dismissed Stanton.

Johnson named Grant secretary.

The removal of Stanton was stopped by Congress. An act stated that removals from office were controlled by Congress.

Grant quickly left office. President Johnson was impeached, but he was not found guilty.

After the split with Johnson, Grant joined the Republican Party. He received its nomination for president in 1868.

Grant ran against Horatio Seymour, the former governor of New York.

Grant became the eighteenth president of the United States with 214 electoral votes. He was the youngest president at the time at the age of 46.

Some of his appointments were good choices, like Hamilton Fish for secretary of state. Fish settled a treaty with Great Britain in 1871 that paid the United States money for damage caused by British-built ships used during the Civil War.

Grant's presidency had many troubles. His military background was different from politics.

There was also Ely S. Parker, a Seneca Indian who became Commissioner of Indian Affairs.

However, Grant also gave positions to people who gave him gifts or were close friends or family.

Mrs. Grant also caused trouble to his term. She redecorated the White House with expensive items and held fancy dinner parties.

Then Nellie Grant, one of Grant's four children, was married at the White House. She became a national spectacle.

Next, Black Friday caused a financial panic on September 24, 1869. During the Civil War and the Reconstruction, the U.S. government issued a large amount of money. People believed that the government would buy back the "greenbacks" with gold.

James Fisk and Jay Gould wanted to make money from the situation. They bought large amounts of gold, saying that the government would not put its gold reserves for sale. This caused gold prices to rise and stocks to drop.

After Grant realized what had happened, the government sold $4 million in gold. This caused the price to go down. Although Grant was not directly involved in the scandal, he was blamed for the crisis.

Gold Speculation

Grant supported the Force Acts, which upheld the rights of all citizens to vote. These acts led to the Fifteenth Amendment to the Constitution. This amendment keeps any government in the United States from denying a citizen the right to vote based on that citizen's race, color, or previous condition of servitude.

However, Grant did not hold up this right. Many groups, such as the Ku Klux Klan, formed to scare African-American voters.

Scholars believe the amendment also led to the segregation that lasted into the 1960s. Despite these problems, Grant easily won reelection in 1872. He defeated Horace Greeley.

Blacks

Whites only

Chapter 6:
A Second Term

In Grant's second term, scandals continued to follow his administration. One was the Credit Mobilier scandal.

This scandal was caused by illegal stock-buying and fraud with the Union Pacific Railroad. Many people were involved, including Grant's first vice president, Schuyler Colfax.

Many people working for Grant were let go for bribery and fraud.

There was also the Whiskey Ring scandal. During this scandal, government officials helped distillers avoid paying taxes.

Finally, a safe burglary conspiracy happened. Corrupt building contractors in Washington DC tried to open a safe that had damaging evidence inside.

Grant was never found to be involved in the scandals. But he did support his staff and family. This reflected poorly on him and made him unpopular.

He ended his second term mostly in disgrace.

FAILURES HAVE BEEN ERRORS OF JUDGMENT, NOT OF INTENT.

Upon leaving office, Ulysses and Julia toured the world. Grant was treated like a hero wherever he went. The couple visited Queen Victoria of England, Emperor Meiji of Japan, and Otto Von Bismarck of Germany.

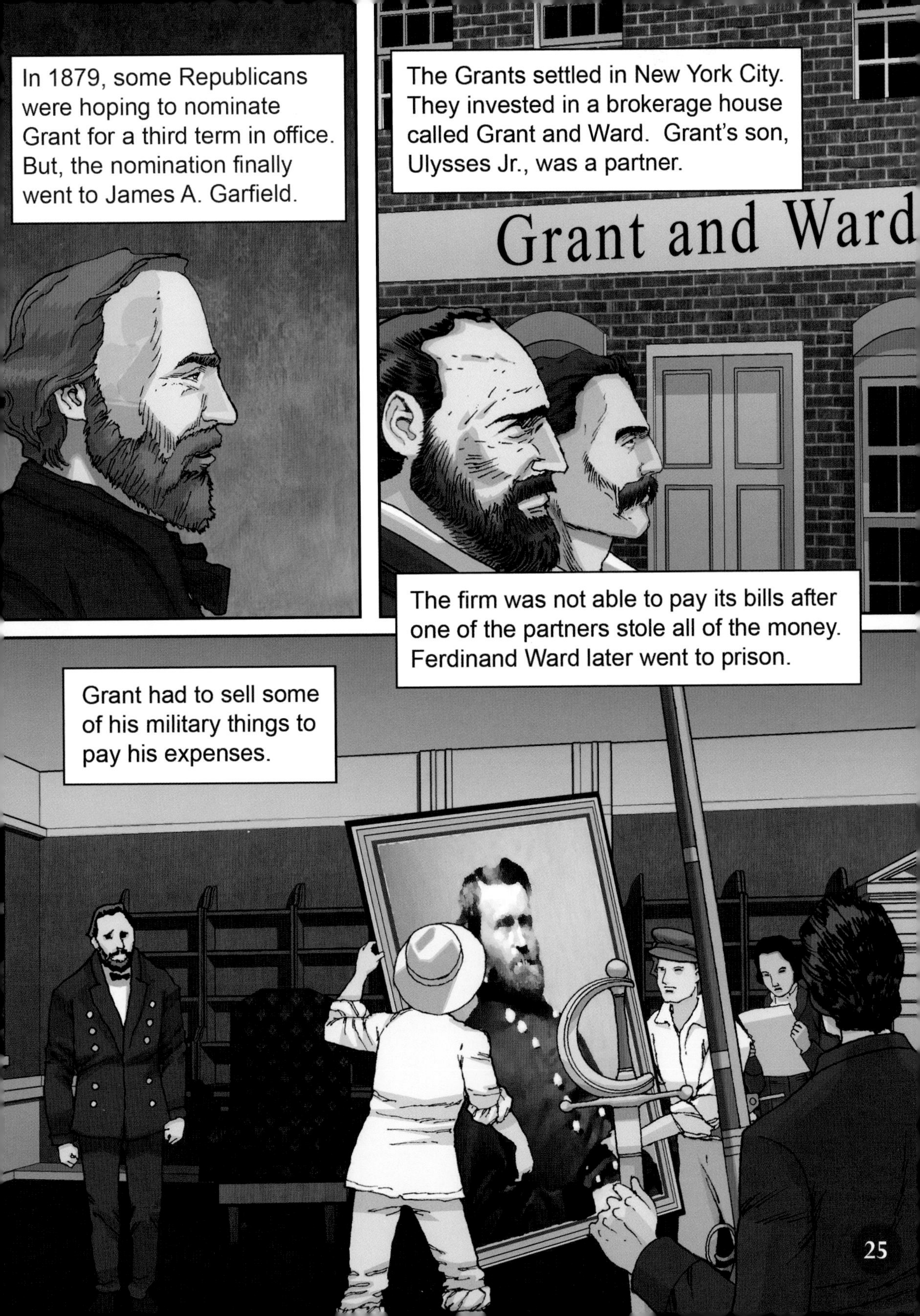
In 1879, some Republicans were hoping to nominate Grant for a third term in office. But, the nomination finally went to James A. Garfield.
The Grants settled in New York City. They invested in a brokerage house called Grant and Ward. Grant's son, Ulysses Jr., was a partner.
Grant and Ward
The firm was not able to pay its bills after one of the partners stole all of the money. Ferdinand Ward later went to prison.
Grant had to sell some of his military things to pay his expenses.

Now nearly poor, Grant began to write a memoir. He hoped to sell it to provide for his family.

Mark Twain helped him publish the book, *Personal Memoirs*. It was a great success.

While Grant was writing his book, he had found out he had throat cancer.

Grant passed away on July 23, 1885, a week after he finished the book.

Grant was temporarily placed in a vault before going to his tomb in 1897. Grant's tomb is in Manhattan. It has two large statues that represent victory and peace. They support a granite block containing his words, "Let us have peace."

Name - Ulysses S. Grant   Born - April 27, 1822

Wife - Julia Boggs Dent (1826–1902)   Children - 4

Political Party - Republican

Age at Inauguration - 46   Years Served - 1869–1877

Vice Presidents - Schuyler Colfax, Henry Wilson

Died - July 23, 1885, age 63

President Grant's Cabinet

First term - March 4, 1869–March 4, 1873
State – Elihu B. Washburne; Hamilton Fish (from March 17, 1869)

Treasury – George S. Boutwell

War – John A. Rawlins; William T. Sherman (from September 11, 1869); William W. Belknap (from November 1, 1869)

Navy – Adolph E. Borie; George M. Robeson (from June 25, 1869)

Attorney General – Ebenezer R. Hoar; Amos T. Akerman (from July 8, 1870); George H. Williams (from January 10, 1872)

Interior – Jacob D. Cox; Columbus Delano (from November 1, 1870)

Second term - March 4, 1873–March 4, 1877
State – Hamilton Fish

Treasury – William A. Richardson; Benjamin H. Bristow (from June 4, 1874); Lot M. Morrill (from July 7, 1876)

War – William W. Belknap; Alphonso Taft (from March 11, 1876); James D. Cameron (from June 1, 1876)

Navy – George M. Robeson

Attorney General – George H. Williams; Edward Pierrepont (from May 15, 1875); Alphonso Taft (from June 1, 1876)

Interior – Columbus Delano; Zachariah Chandler (from October 19, 1875)

The Office of the President

• To be president, a person must meet three requirements. He or she must be at least 35 years old and a natural-born U.S. citizen. A candidate must also have lived in the United States for at least 14 years.

• The U.S. presidential election is an indirect election. Voters from each state elect representatives called electors for the Electoral College. The number of electors is based on population. Each elector pledges to cast their vote for the candidate who receives the highest number of popular votes in their state. A candidate must receive the majority of Electoral College votes to win.

• Each president may be elected to two four-year terms. The presidential election is held on the Tuesday after the first Monday in November. The president is sworn in on January 20 of the following year.

• While in office, the president receives a salary of $400,000 each year. He or she lives in the White House and has 24-hour Secret Service protection. When the president leaves office, he or she receives Secret Service protection for ten more years. He or she also receives a yearly pension of $191,300 and funding for office space, supplies, and staff.

Timeline

1822 - Ulysses S. Grant was born on April 27 in Point Pleasant, Ohio.

1839 - Grant began his schooling at West Point.

1843 - Grant graduated from West Point in June. In September, he was assigned to the 4th U.S. Infantry.

1846 to 1848 - Grant served in the Mexican War; he received two awards for bravery.

1848 - Grant married Julia Boggs Dent on August 22.

1854 - Grant left the army and returned to St. Louis, Missouri, to farm.

1861 - In April the Civil War began. Grant was made colonel over the 21st Illinois Volunteers. On August 7, Lincoln named Grant brigadier general of the volunteers of Cairo, Illinois.

1863 - Grant captured Vicksburg on July 4. On November 25, he won the Battle of Chattanooga.

1865 - General Robert E. Lee surrendered to Grant at Appomattox Court House on April 9.

1868 - Grant was voted president in November.

1872 - Grant won a second term.

1877 - Grant retired from office.

1884 - Grant was diagnosed with throat cancer.

1885 - Grant died on July 23.

Web Sites

To learn more about Ulysses S. Grant, visit ABDO Publishing Group online at **www.abdopublishing.com**. Web sites about Grant are featured on our Book Links page. These links are routinely monitored and updated to provide the most current information available.

Glossary

assassinate - to murder a very important person, usually for political reasons.

bribery - the act of taking money or a favor in order to influence a person in position of trust.

Confederate States of America - the government of the states of North Carolina, South Carolina, Georgia, Florida, Alabama, Louisiana, Mississippi, Texas, Virginia, Tennessee, and Arkansas, which left the Union in 1860 and 1861. It is also called the Confederacy.

conspiracy - the act of joining a secret agreement to do an unlawful or wrongful act.

crisis - an unstable or crucial time.

distiller - a person who makes a liquid or other substance pure by heating and cooling it.

fraud - an act of deceiving or misrepresenting.

impeach - to charge a public official for crime or misconduct in office.

Mexican War - from 1846 to 1848. A war fought between the United States and Mexico.

nomination - the act of proposing a candidtate for election to an office.

Reconstruction - the period after the American Civil War from 1865 to 1877. During this time, the Southern states were restored to the Union.

regiment - a military unit consisting of a number of battalions.

Republican - a member of the Republican political party during the American Civil War. At that time, Republicans against slavery were known as Radical Republicans.

scandal - an action that shocks people and disgraces those connected with it.

segregation - the separation of an individual or a group from a larger group.

siege - a military blockade of a city.

spectacle - something seen as unusual, notable, or entertaining.

strategy - a careful plan or method.

unconditional surrender - to completely give up something.

Union - the states that remained in the United States during the Civil War.

Index